What's in this book

This book belongs to

_____

滑板不见了！
The skateboard is missing!

学习内容 Contents

沟通 Communication

说出房间的名称
Say the names of rooms

说说家中的房间
Talk about the rooms in a home

生词 New words

★	卧室	bedroom
★	洗手间	bathroom
★	书房	study
★	厨房	kitchen
★	客厅	living room
★	家	home
	花园	garden
	外面	outside
	里面	inside
	滑板	skateboard
	很	very

句式 Sentence patterns

客厅很整洁。
The living room is very tidy.

文化 Cultures

中国的四合院
Traditional Chinese house

跨学科学习 Project

量度、绘画、描述房间
Measure, draw and describe a room

Get ready

1 Which is your favourite room at home?

2 Do you like Hao Hao's home?

3 Where do you think Hao Hao put his skateboard?

huá bǎn
滑板

浩浩的滑板不见了，他很着急。

wò shì
卧室

shū fáng
书房

xǐ shǒu jiān
洗手间

卧室、书房、洗手间里
面都没有滑板。

chú fáng
厨房

爸爸在厨房，他说："别急，滑板一定在家里面。"

客厅很整洁，里面也没有滑板。

"不要在家里面玩，到外面去。"妈妈说。

huā yuán

花园

"我知道它在哪里了，
它在花园！"浩浩说。

Let's think

1 Hao Hao looked for his skateboard at home. Recall the story and number the rooms and places in order.

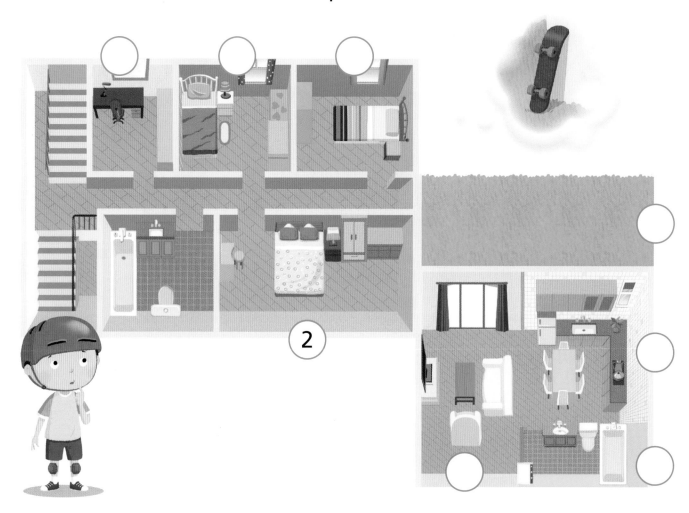

2 Which activity is more fun? What should the children wear? Discuss with your friend.

New words

1 Learn the new words.

书房

外面

里面

洗手间

卧室

厨房

客厅

花园

我很喜欢我的家。

滑板

2 Match the words to the pictures. Write the letters.

a 书房   b 客厅   c 厨房   d 洗手间

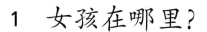

03 **1** Listen and circle the correct letters.

04 **2** Look at the pictures. Listen to the sto

1 女孩在哪里？

   a 卧室

   b 客厅

   c 书房

2 洗手间在哪里？

   a 客厅后面

   b 书房前面

   c 卧室后面

3 铅笔在哪里？

   a 书房外面

   b 书房里面

   c 洗手间里面

① 爸爸在家吗？

②

在，他在客厅里面。

③ 很好，很好。你呢？

…nd say.

这个家很大，很好看，也很整洁，是吗？

爷爷在哪里？奶奶呢？

谁在书房？谁在卧室？

洗手间里面有人吗？

Task

Draw a floor plan of your home and introduce your home to your friend.

我的家有三个卧室，一个洗手间。客厅和厨房很大，花园在外面。

这是我的家。这是……

Game

Listen to your teacher.
Point to the correct rooms.

爸爸去书房。

妈妈在……

……

Song

🎧 05 Listen and sing.

这是我的家，
外面是花园，
里面是房间，
上面是卧室，
下面是客厅，
家里还有厨房、书房和洗手间。
我爱我的家。

课堂用语 Classroom language

请再说一次。
Say it one more time, please.

1 Learn and trace the stroke.

弯钩

2 Learn the component. Trace 宀 to complete the characters.

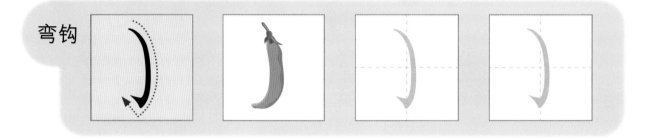

宀 窗 家 室 客

3 Colour the roof red and 丿 in the characters green.

猴 狮 猫 狗

16

4 Trace and write the characters.

丶 宀 宀 宀 宁 宁 家 家 家

家 家

丶 宀 宀 宀 宀 宀 客 客 客

客 客

5 Write and say.

这是我们的 ☐ 。 这是 ☐ 厅。

Cultures

1 Do you know what a *Siheyuan* is? Read and learn about it.

A *Siheyuan* is a traditional type of house with a courtyard surrounded by houses on all four sides. It is also known as a courtyard house. *Siheyuan* can still be found in Bejing.

2 Listen to your teacher. Point to the pictures and the words at the same time.

卧室　　客厅　　家　　书房　　厨房

Project

Measure and draw your room. Talk about it with your friend.

你的卧室很整洁。

门很高，是红色的。

我很喜欢你的卧室。

床很矮，也是红色的。

我的卧室	颜色 colour	长 length	宽 width	高 height
门		_____ cm	_____ cm	_____ cm
床		_____ cm	_____ cm	_____ cm
桌子		_____ cm	_____ cm	_____ cm

19

温习 Checkpoint

1 Match the rooms to the words. Write the letters.
Play hide-and-seek with your friend.

Trace the character.

我在家里面。

我不在书房。

我也不在卧室。

我在沙发后面。

我在哪里？

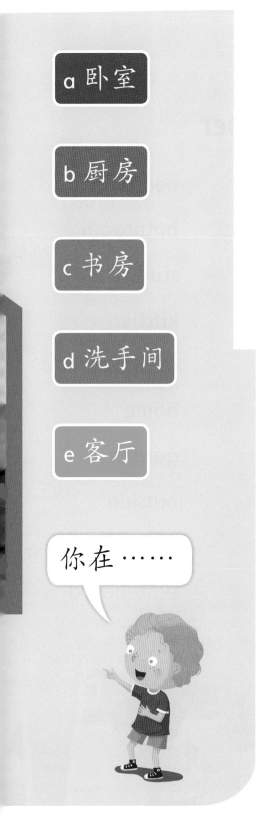

a 卧室

b 厨房

c 书房

d 洗手间

e 客厅

你在……

2 Work with your friend. Colour the stars and the chillies.

Words and sentences	说	读	写
卧室	☆	☆	🌶
洗手间	☆	☆	🌶
书房	☆	☆	🌶
厨房	☆	☆	🌶
客厅	☆	☆	🌶
家	☆	☆	☆
花园	☆	🌶	🌶
外面	☆	🌶	🌶
里面	☆	🌶	🌶
滑板	☆	🌶	🌶
很	☆	🌶	🌶
爸爸在厨房。	☆	☆	🌶
客厅很整洁。	☆	🌶	🌶

Say the names of rooms	☆
Talk about rooms at home	☆

3 What does your teacher say?

分享 Sharing

Words I remember

卧室	wò shì	bedroom
洗手间	xǐ shǒu jiān	bathroom
书房	shū fáng	study
厨房	chú fáng	kitchen
客厅	kè tīng	living room
家	jiā	home
花园	huā yuán	garden
外面	wài miàn	outside
里面	lǐ miàn	inside
滑板	huá bǎn	skateboard
很	hěn	very

Other words

不见	bù jiàn	missing
着急	zháo jí	to worry
别	bié	do not
一定	yī dìng	certainly
整洁	zhěng jié	tidy
到	dào	to go to
不要	bù yào	do not
知道	zhī dào	to know

Oxford University Press is a department of the University of Oxford.
It furthers the University's objective of excellence in research, scholarship,
and education by publishing worldwide. Oxford is a registered trade mark of
Oxford University Press in the UK and in certain other countries

Published in Hong Kong by
Oxford University Press (China) Limited
39th Floor, One Kowloon, 1 Wang Yuen Street, Kowloon Bay,
Hong Kong

First Edition published in 2017

Illustrated by Anne Lee and Wildman

Photographs for reproduction permitted by Dreamstime.com

China National Publications Import & Export (Group) Corporation is an authorized distributor of
Oxford Elementary Chinese.

Please contact content@cnpiec.com.cn or 86-10-65856782

ISBN: 978-0-19-082200-2

10 9 8 7 6 5 4 3